The Poetry Coaster

A Loop-de-Loop of Classic Poetic Forms

Poetry by Lucas Raney

Illustrated by Mason Bell

Two Turkey Publishing, LLC

2001 Timberloch Place Suite 500, The Woodlands, Texas 77380

Names: Raney, Lucas, author. | Bell, Mason, 1975- illustrator.

Title: The poetry coaster : a loop–de–loop of classic poetic forms/ poetry by Lucas Raney ; illustrated by

Mason Bell.

Description: The Woodlands, Texas : Two Turkey Publishing, LLC,[2025] | Audience: ages 9–16, grades 4th

to 9th. | Summary:"The Poetry Coaster" is a hilarious roller coaster-themed poetry collection by ten-

year-old Lucas.Using forms like diamante, haiku, acrostic, and more, he captures the thrills, spills,

and snack stand mishaps of coaster life. Each poem blends humor and heart, from personal

reflections to wild metaphors and persuasive arguments for loving loops. This laugh–out–loud ride

through rhyme and imagination is poetry with a twist!.––Publisher.

Identifiers: ISBN: 9798986606699 (paperback)

Subjects: LCSH: Roller coasters––Juvenile poetry. | Humorouspoetry. | Young adult poetry. | CYAC: Roller

coasters––Poetry. |Poetry. | LCGFT: Poetry. | Children's stories. | BISAC: JUVENILEFICTION /

Concepts /Language. | POETRY / General.

Classification: LCC: PZ7.1.B45232 P64 2025 | DDC: [Fic]––dc23

“I dedicate this book to my father, Douglas Raney.

Had he not taken me to my first rollercoaster ride on the Shockwave, I would not have written this, and you would not be reading it.”

-Lucas Raney

You've got your ticket,
and now the fun begins!

Lucas will be your riding buddy
throughout the immersive pages of
this book, putting the Thrill in the
Hill and the Whip in the Dip.

So pull that seatbelt tight and
grab the handrail as we roar
through ten classic forms of
awesome poetry!

Diamante
Haiku
Two Tone
Personal
Persuasive
I Am
How-To
Acrostic
Free Verse
Extended Metaphor

Diamante Poem

A Diamante poem has seven lines, forms a diamond shape, and is named after the Spanish word diamante.

It follows a specific pattern to compare two opposite things or to describe one thing in more detail.

Here's the pattern:

Noun
Adjective, Adjective
Verb, Verb, Verb
Noun, Noun, Noun, Noun
Verb, Verb, Verb
Adjective, Adjective
Noun

Diamante

Rollercoaster,
Loud, Rickety,
Dropping, Screaming, Climbing,
Track, Loop, Plunge, Splash,
Bending, Twisting, Turning,
Fast, Wet,
Waterslide

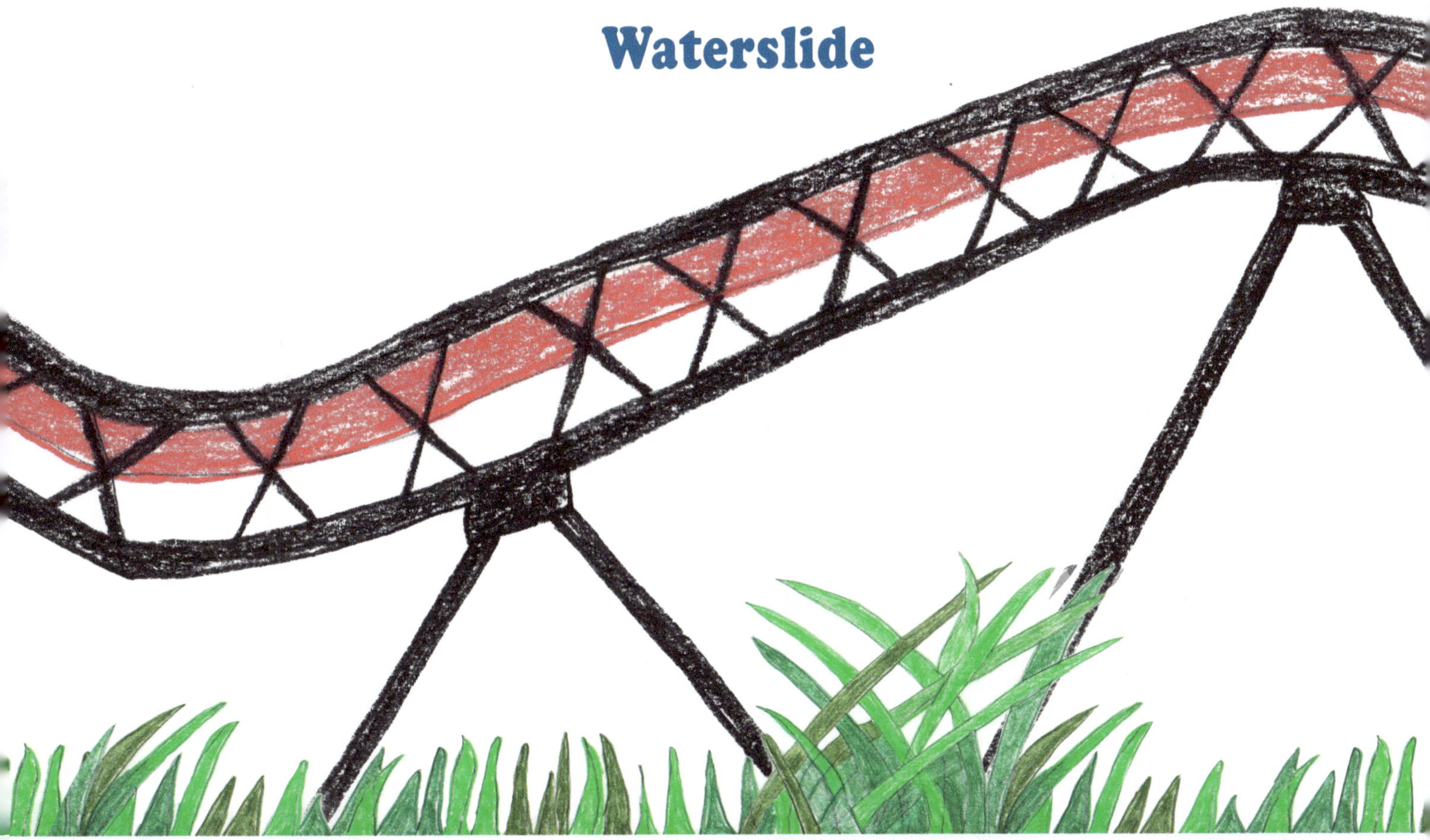

Haiku Poem

A Haiku is a short,
three-line poem that
originated in Japan.

The first line has
5 syllables, the second
has 7, and the third has 5.

Haikus often focus on nature
or simple moments in life.

Here's the pattern:

5 Syllables
7 Syllables
5 Syllables

Haiku

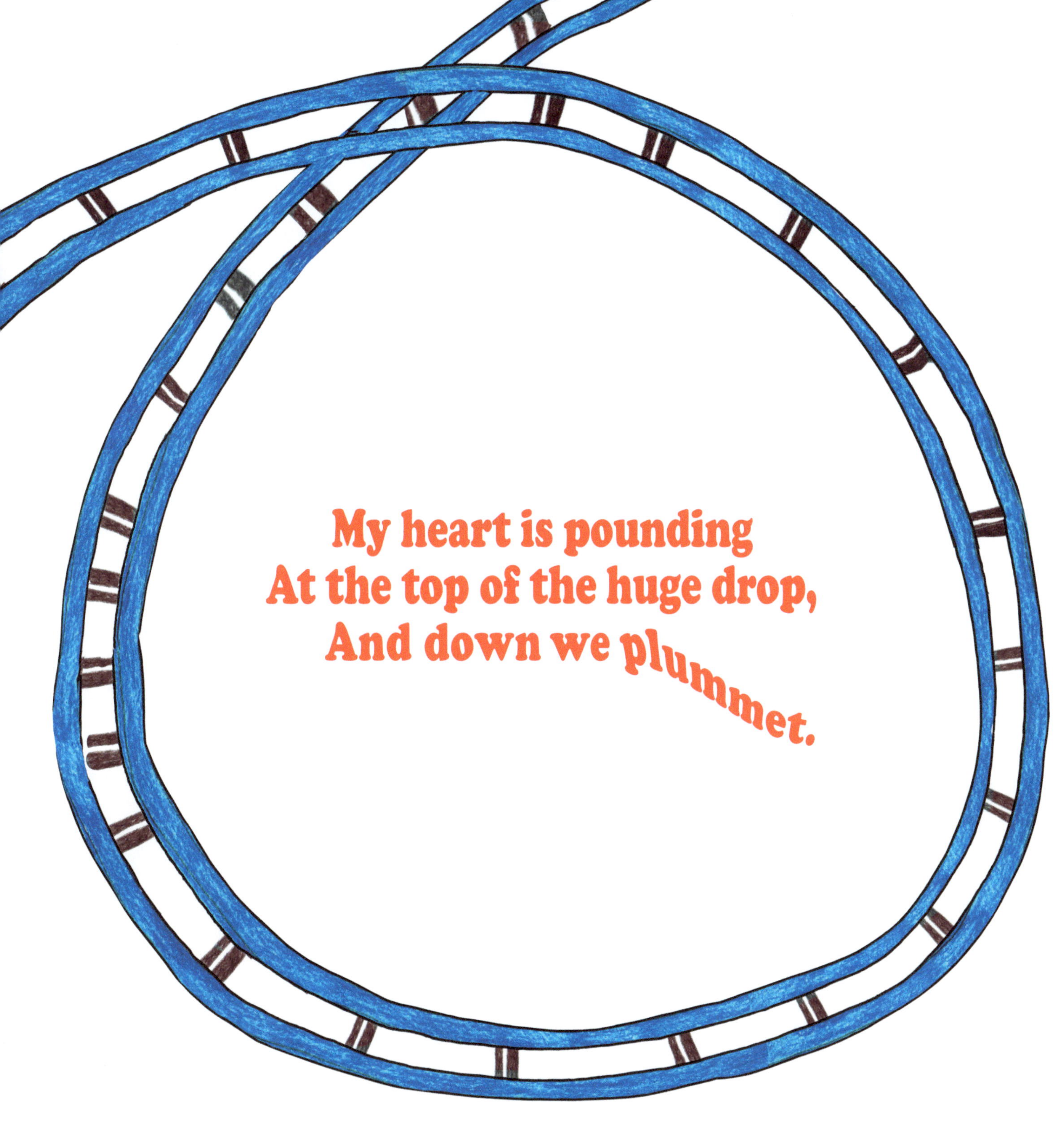

My heart is pounding
At the top of the huge drop,
And down we plummet.

Two Tone Poem

Two Tone poetry
shows two different moods,
ideas, or voices. It might
compare opposites like love
and hate or hope and fear,
switching topics between
lines or sections.

Two Tone poems generally
do not have patterns.

Two Tone
poems rely
on contrasting
ideas and
emotions to
make a poem
powerful and
interesting
to read.

Two Tone

When I step into the seat I'm a pale white,
Waiting for what horrors lay ahead.
I can see the first hill go Up, Up, Up,
Straight into the sky.

Soon, though, I'm a vibrant red,
What with the blood rushing to my head.
As we twist and turn and Loop-de-Loop,
I scream in delight.

Afterwards, I'm a pale green-
I think you know why!

Personal Poem

A Personal poem allows the writer to talk about their own life, feelings, or thoughts.

It's like writing a poem about something important to you like a memory, a strong emotion, or special event.

Personal poems are often deep and honest, helping the reader understand the writer's feelings.

Personal

My name is Lucas Raney.
My person is content with his name.
I would most likely become the
Southwest Flying Tree Octopus.

The object inside me is a rollercoaster.
I love the word on my forehead.
The word on my forehead
is thrill.
I love the smell of
burnt rubber.
I like races.

My favorite time of day is night.
You can't see where the rollercoaster is going.
If my hands could speak, they'd say,

I remember being
on the top of the
first giant hill.

Turkey!

Persuasive Poem

A Persuasive poem tries to convince the reader to think, feel, or act a certain way.

It uses strong words, emotions, and facts to change the reader's mind or inspire them to do something.

A Persuasive poem doesn't have a specific pattern, but can use rhyme, rhythm, or a certain number of lines in each stanza to make the poem sound strong and memorable.

Persuasive

Come on! Get in!
The door is wide open!
What, you say? You won't?
I don't see why you don't!

It's not safe? That's not true!
Of all other times, why so blue?
You have a sturdy handgrip,
And your seatbelt won't rip.
So why isn't *it* safe?
It's at a safe place!

I Am Poem

An I Am poem allows the
writer to share their
thoughts, dreams, and fears
creatively.

By expressing what they
think or feel, the poem gives
the reader insight into the
writer's world.

These four phrases are often used at the start of each line:

I am
I feel
I wonder
I dream

I AM

I am speed loving and daring.
I wonder how to build rollercoasters.
I hear a loud roar.
I see the ground coming closer.
I want to go up.
I am speed loving and daring.

I pretend to be exiting the ride.
I feel fear and excitment.
I touch the handgrip.
I worry about a malfunction.
I cry about a crash.
I am speed loving and daring.

I understand I am going to get off.
I say it is perfectly safe.
I dream of getting off.
I am speed loving and daring.

How-To Poem

A How-To poem gives
step-by-step directions
for doing something, like
baking a cake or being a
good friend—but in
a creative way.

It can be serious
or silly. The poem might
sound like a recipe or
instructions.

How-To poems have no special pattern, but most poets use rhythm or repetition to create interest.

How to Ride a Rollercoaster

1. Do not eat before you ride.

2. Wait in line patiently.

3. Locate trashcan in advance.

4. Look terrified.

5. Be anxious going uphill.

6. Scream throughout ride.

7. Put hands up in the air.

8. Exit to the right.

9. Relocate trashcan.

How-To

Acrostic Poem

An Acrostic poem uses the first letter of each line to spell out a word or phrase when read vertically.

This word or phrase often serves as the poem's theme or title.

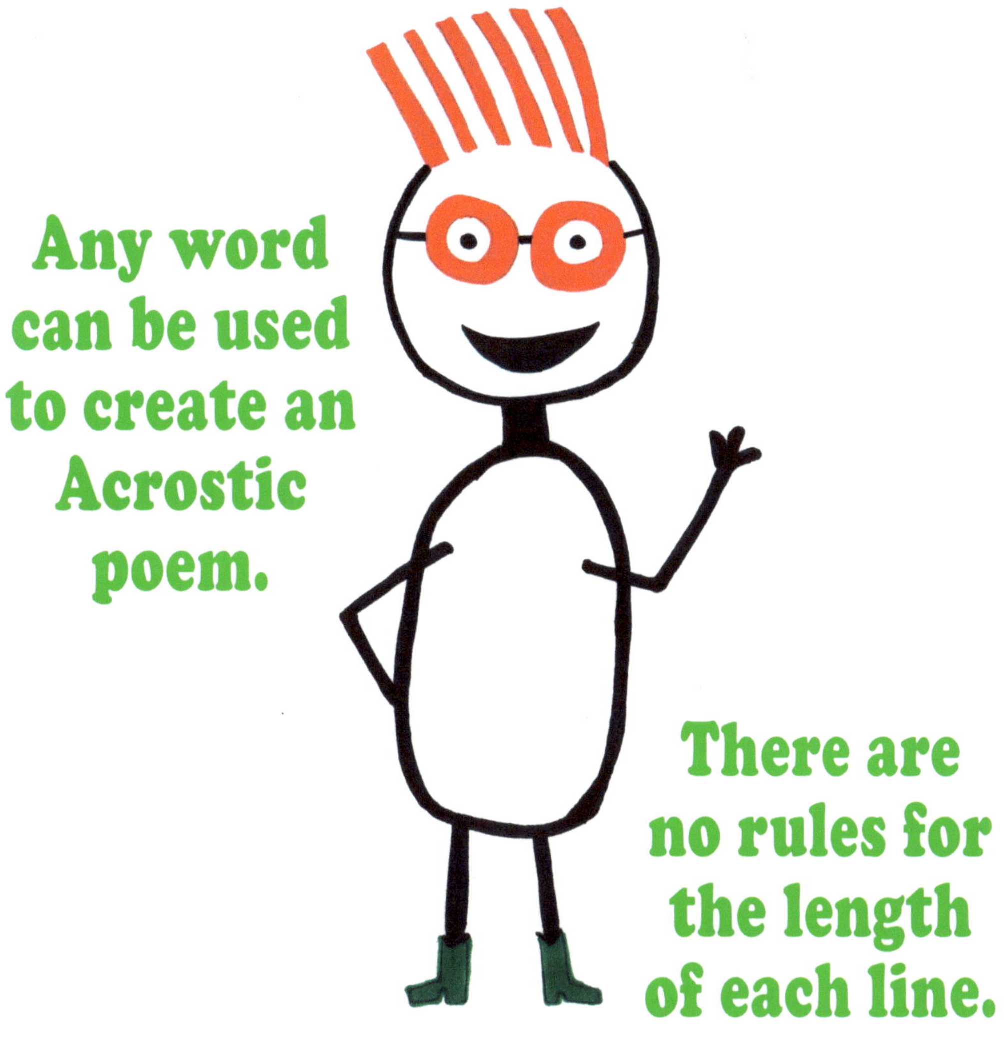
Any word
can be used
to create an
Acrostic
poem.

There are
no rules for
the length
of each line.

Acrostic

Riding up and down

Over the hills and

Lumps of the really

Loud coaster can

Eventually make your

Rear-end hurt from

Collapsing in your seat

Over a bump or turn

Around too fast.

Smooth coasters

Try not to do that

Every so often. It

Really helps.

Free Verse Poem

A Free Verse poem
doesn't follow rules like
rhyme or rhythm.

It sounds more like
normal speech, but it's still
creative and full of feelings
or imagery.

Poets can
choose how
long the lines are
and how the poem
looks, giving them
more freedom
to express
themselves.

Free Verse

As it rolls around
Like an untamed beast,
It roars through the air,
Public adding to it.

While it loops in groups,
People throw up their arms
Screaming in delight.

Extended Metaphor Poem

An Extended Metaphor
poem compares one thing
to another in a creative way,
keeping that comparison
going through the
whole poem.

It's more elaborate
and sustained than a
simple metaphor.

Extended Metaphors do not have a set pattern, but often use strong images and creative language.

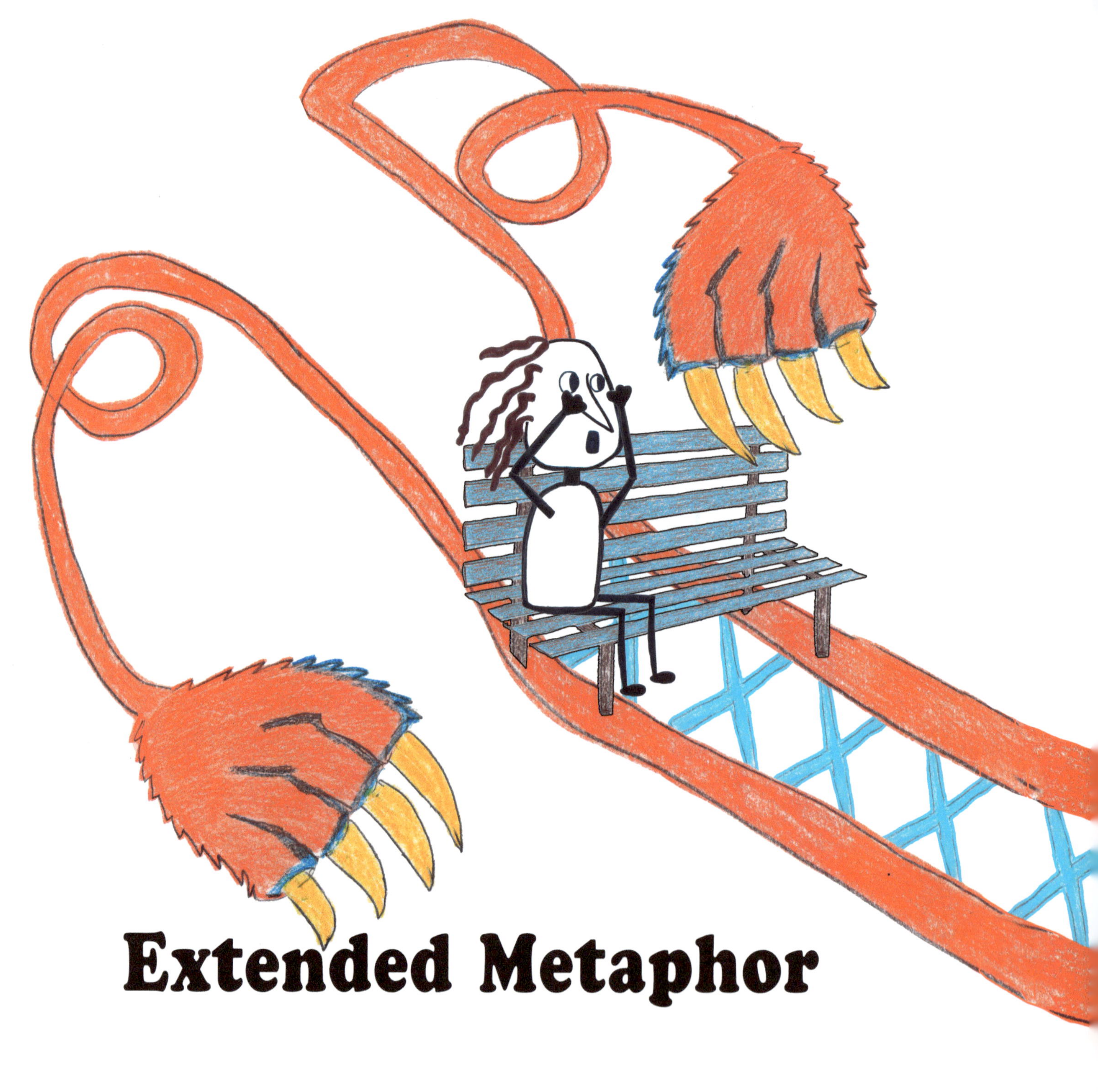

Extended Metaphor

A rollercoaster is a thing with benches,
Benches that move at high speeds.
They yell up and down hills,
Innocent civilians screaming with it.

As they move in obtuse ways,
They bring out the fear in people,
But also the delight
As it twists and turns.

When the beast shows his wrath,
You cannot help but hint a smile
As it tickles you in the strangest way;
Conveying fears into the day.

The Ride May Be Over... But the Thrill Never Ends!

From Loop-de-Loops of Diamante to the soaring heights of Extended Metaphor, you've just coasted through ten thrilling forms of poetry—with Lucas riding shotgun the whole way.

But just because we're rolling into the station doesn't mean the fun has to stop! Hop back in line anytime. Re-read your favorite twists and turns or buckle up for another full run.

Stay twisty,
rhyme boldly,
and speed on!

Meet the Poet

I am Lucas Raney. I chose a rollercoaster theme because I love the thrill of moving at high speeds, and rollercoasters seem to supply that.

Some of my hobbies are experimenting with physics on a game that I like and acting in school plays.

I do not like seafood.

Meet the Illustrator

I am Mason Bell. I also love rollercoasters, but instead of crafting poetry, I write children's books about adventure and friendship.

Some of my hobbies outside of writing and illustrating books are gardening, photography, and watching wild animals do crazy stuff.

I do not like liver.

Leave your super-special review
of this book and
help fill every seat on this train!